SMART STRUCTURES

CANALS AND AQUEDUCTS

Julie Richards

This edition first published in 2004 in the United States of America by Smart Apple Media.

Smart Apple Media
1980 Lookout Drive
North Mankato
Minnesota 56003

Library of Congress Cataloging-in-Publication Data

Richards, Julie.
    Canals and aqueducts / by Julie Richards.
    p. cm. — (Smart structures)

    Includes index.
    Summary: Describes different kinds of canals and aqueducts built, the methods and materials of their construction, and amazing or disastrous examples.

    ISBN 1-58340-347-7
    1. Canals—Design and construction—Juvenile literature. 2. Aqueducts—Design and construction—Juvenile literature. [1. Canals—Design and construction. 2. Aqueducts—Design and construction.] I. Title.
    TC745.R5 2003
    627'.13—dc21   2002044614

First Edition
9 8 7 6 5 4 3 2 1

First published in 2003 by
MACMILLAN EDUCATION AUSTRALIA PTY LTD
627 Chapel Street, South Yarra, Australia 3141

Associated companies and representatives throughout the world.

Copyright © Julie Richards 2003

Edited by Anna Fern
Text design by Cristina Neri, Canary Graphic Design
Cover design by Cristina Neri, Canary Graphic Design
Layout by Nina Sanadze
Illustrations and map by Margaret Hastie, IKON Computergraphics
Photo research by Legend Images

Printed in Thailand

Acknowledgements
The author and the publisher are grateful to the following for permission to reproduce copyright material:

Cover photograph: Roquefort Aqueduct, France, courtesy of Getty Images.

ANT Photo Library, p. 19; Australian Picture Library/Corbis, pp. 5 (top right), 18, 24, 26, 27; Eye Ubiquitous, pp. 13, 16; Getty Images, pp. 1, 5 (top left & bottom), 8, 12, 17, 22, 23, 25; © 2003 Mark A. Johnson, p. 9; Legend Images, p. 4; © 2002 The LEGO Group, p. 30; Mary Evans Picture Library, p. 20; Photolibrary.com, p. 28; Reuters, pp. 14, 15; Ted Waddell, United States National Park Service, p. 11.

While every care has been taken to trace and acknowledge copyright, the publisher tenders their apologies for any accidental infringement where copyright has proved untraceable. Where the attempt has been unsuccessful, the publisher welcomes information that would redress the situation.

CONTENTS

KEY WORDS

When a word is printed in **bold** you can look up its meaning in the key words box on the same page. You can also look up the meaning of words in the glossary on page 31.

CANALS AND AQUEDUCTS AS STRUCTURES

A **structure** is made up of many different parts joined together. The shapes of the parts and the way they are joined together help a structure to stand up and do the job for which it has been designed. The **materials** used to make a structure can be made stronger or weaker, depending on their shape and how they are put together.

For as long as people have used water as a form of transportation or needed to move water from one place to another, they have built water-filled structures called canals and aqueducts.

Canals and aqueducts are useful for:

- bringing freshwater from mountain rivers and springs into towns and cities
- watering crops
- carrying dirty wastewater away
- draining swamps and low-lying land so that it can be used for other things
- removing stormwater to prevent flooding
- providing a source of water to run water-powered **mills** and machines
- generating electricity
- providing inland cities with a link to the sea
- joining ports and rivers, lakes, and seas so that journeys by water are shorter, easier, and safer, and goods can be moved quickly and cheaply
- enabling boats to bypass dangerous coastline, steep waterfalls, very shallow water, or fast currents
- boating vacations and fun.

◀ Rivers are not always the easiest way to transport goods or move water to where it is needed.

KEY WORDS

structure something that is made up of many parts joined together

materials anything used to make a structure

mills buildings where grain is crushed to make flour

Types of canals and aqueducts

Most canals are open structures and are built in the same way. The size of a canal and where it is built depends on what it is needed for.

An aqueduct is the name given to anything that carries water from its source to where it is needed. Modern aqueducts include underground water and **sewage** tunnels. Aqueduct is also the name given to a bridge that carries water above a road, river, or railroad, or across a valley between hills.

These canals and aqueducts are built for different purposes.

This canal allows large ships to travel across land between oceans, making the journey shorter and safer.

Canals like this one were built to transport goods from factories to shops during the 1700s, before railroads or motor vehicles were invented. The **barges** were pulled by horses.

Stone aqueducts like this were built by the ancient Romans. They carried water from mountain streams across valleys and into towns and cities.

This stormwater drain in Los Angeles, California, prevents flooding during rain storms.

LOOKING AT CANALS AND AQUEDUCTS

If you look very closely at a canal or aqueduct, you will notice:

- the different parts which have been joined together to build the canal or aqueduct
- the shapes of these parts.

Tunnels, **cuttings**, **embankments**, **locks**, bridges, and aqueducts are all part of a canal system. It is important that the different parts of the canal or aqueduct are made into the right shapes and joined together in the right way, otherwise the canal will not be **watertight**, and the weight of the water and the boats traveling on it will not be properly supported.

KEY WORDS

cuttings passages that have been dug through a hill

embankments human-made mounds of earth that support a canal

locks steps on a canal that let boats move uphill or downhill

watertight not leaking

Canal and aqueduct shapes

Some shapes are stronger than others, but they all have their breaking point. An arch is one of the strongest shapes used to build big structures.

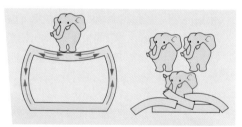

Rectangle

One elephant on a rectangle makes the top side bend. The weight of three elephants causes the top side to break.

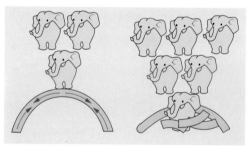

Arch

The weight of three elephants on an arch spreads along the curve to the ground below. The weight of six elephants causes the sides to spread apart and collapse.

Triangle

The weight of six elephants on a triangle causes the two top sides to squeeze together and the bottom side to pull apart. The triangle is the strongest shape, but a herd of elephants makes the bottom side stretch so much that it snaps in half.

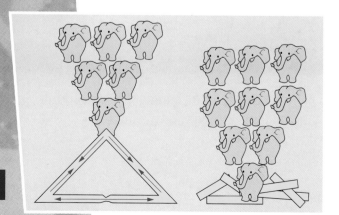

What shapes do canal structures use?

All canal structures use the same basic shapes for the canal **channel**, tunnels, cuttings, bridges, and aqueducts. If you sliced across a canal and looked at the end, you would see that the canal itself has sloping sides and is wider at the top than it is at the bottom. This canal shape is called a trapezium. The trapezium is the right shape to keep the water inside the canal channel and to stop the banks from collapsing.

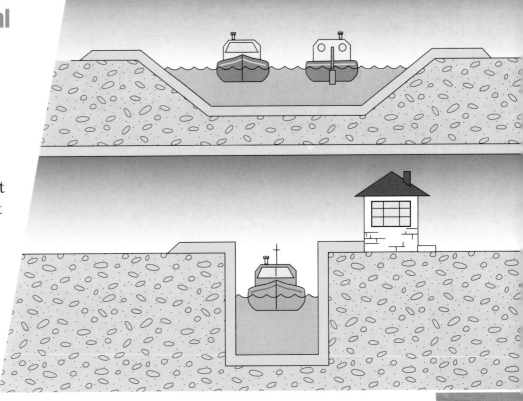

All canals are wider at the top than the bottom and have sloping sides. Where a boat needs to tie up at the side of the canal, the sides are **vertical**.

Arches

The tunnels, cuttings, and bridges along a canal are mostly arch-shaped. The aqueducts built by ancient peoples were rows of arches joined together with more arches stacked on top. These aqueducts have survived more than 2,000 years! This shows just how strong the arch shape is.

This section of a canal shows the different shapes of canal structures. ▶

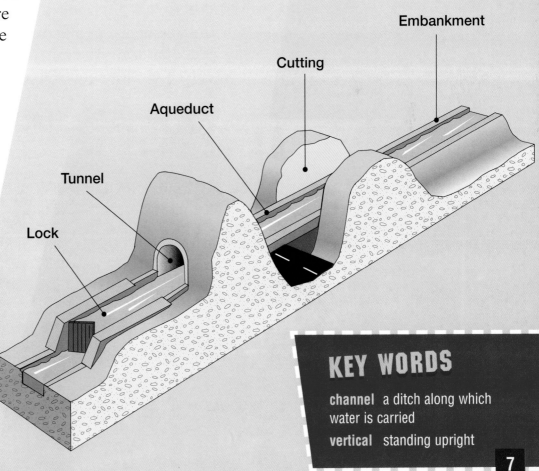

Embankment

Cutting

Aqueduct

Tunnel

Lock

KEY WORDS

channel a ditch along which water is carried

vertical standing upright

THE PARTS OF A CANAL

A canal always stays level, even if the land it is running through is hilly. The different parts of a canal help to keep it level on its journey through the countryside and past anything in its path, such as a road, river, or railroad.

Channels

For most of its length, a canal is a channel in the ground filled with water. Many canals have a towpath alongside the canal bank. Before engines were invented, a very strong horse or a pair of donkeys walked along the towpath, towing the canal boat behind them.

Cuttings and tunnels

Some hills are small and made of soft ground that can be easily cut through by powerful earth-moving and digging equipment. This is called a cutting.

If the hills are too large or made of harder rock, a tunnel will be dug to take the canal channel through.

An embankment is a pile of earth and rock with sloping sides and a flat top. An embankment supports the canal and keeps it level in a hilly area.

KEY WORDS

concrete a building material made by mixing cement and sand or gravel with water

Locks

Canal locks are made up of stone or **concrete** side walls which hold up the ground on each side of the lock. At each end of the lock there are gates to let the water in and out. Locks are like a staircase, allowing boats to move uphill and downhill.

This is a lock. Canal boats use a lock to travel uphill and downhill.

Aqueducts and bridges

Aqueducts are very strong bridges which carry the canal water and the boats on it across valleys and over any rivers, roads, or railroads that may cross its path. Other bridges allow people to walk over the canal. Some bridges are built between buildings.

Venice, Italy, is built on a series of islands. Instead of roads, people travel along canals by gondola or motor boat. There are about 400 bridges, which are used to cross over the canals.

The first aqueducts were stone arches. Stones and bricks were placed around special arch-shaped wooden frames. The last stone to be put into place was the keystone. The keystone sat at the top of the arch and pushed down on the stones next to it. All the stones pushed down on each other. The weight of the arch and anything passing across it was spread along the sides of the arch and down into the ground on either side.

The arch was **reinforced** at the bottom to stop its supporting sides from "doing the splits." Once the keystone was in place, the wooden frame would be removed. The Romans built their famous aqueducts this way, using wooden scaffolding to build the **piers** and wooden cranes to lift the heavy stones. Men ran inside the wheels, allowing the cranes to work.

From about 144 B.C., the Romans built many aqueducts because the drinking water brought up from wells in the ground was not clean enough.

KEY WORDS

gondola a long, narrow boat pushed forward by a pole

reinforced made stronger

piers upright columns on which arches rest

BUILDING MATERIALS

Different building materials are needed for different canal structures. Some canal structures, such as embankments and cuttings, are made from the soil and rock that is removed as the canal channel is dug. Other structures are made from concrete and steel. Early canals were dug by hand until steam-powered shovels were invented in the early 1800s. The earth was taken away in carts pulled by animals.

Concrete

Concrete is a runny mixture of sand, gravel, **cement**, and water. As concrete dries, it hardens and becomes stronger. Concrete hardens in a few hours and takes about a month to reach its maximum strength. Concrete is used to build modern aqueducts and bridges because it can support a much greater weight than the stone and wooden aqueducts and bridges of the past. Some modern canal cargo barges can carry as much as 50 truckloads at once.

Concrete lasts much longer and is easier to look after than wood. Wood cannot be protected from the weather unless it is treated with chemicals. These chemicals can be damaging to the animals, birds, and fish that live in and around the canal.

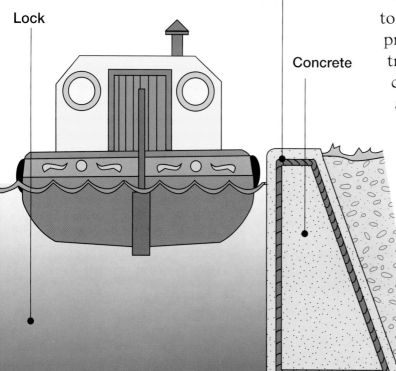

Reinforcing steel

Concrete

Lock

You can see how a concrete lock wall is reinforced by a steel bar.

Concrete is a good building material because it is extremely strong and quite cheap. It can be made and poured at the building site as it is needed. It can also be mixed and poured into molds at a factory and then brought to the site when the builders are ready to use it. Concrete is also used as a lining for tunnels and locks because it is waterproof.

Steel

Steel is an **alloy** made mostly of iron. Steel is used to make lock gates and supports for modern aqueducts and bridges. Steel is immensely strong—a steel cable as thick as your finger could lift a 33-ton (30-t) truck! It is also very light and can stretch.

Bunches of steel bars can be added to concrete, making it stronger and more **flexible**. Making concrete flexible helps prevent it from cracking. The concrete parts of a bridge or aqueduct that will stretch under the weight of water and boats on a canal are made stronger by adding steel.

The Delaware Aqueduct was the first aqueduct to use steel cables to support the weight of the water in the channel. The cables are stretched, which makes them very strong. They support the aqueduct in the same way that a person is supported when they lie in a hammock.

Channel linings

A canal will only stay watertight if the channel is lined with the right material. No lining is necessary in places where the canal goes through solid rock, but some soft rocks have tiny holes which soak up water like sponges. To stop water from leaking out of the canal, a waterproof lining is laid along the channel.

Waterproof linings include:

- clay
- asphalt, a sticky substance made from oil
- polythene, a type of plastic which can be made into thin sheets.

KEY WORDS

alloy a mixture of two or more metals
flexible able to bend without breaking

CANAL DESIGN

Engineers do a lot of research before a canal is designed and built. What they decide to build will depend on what the canal is to be used for and what type of land it will travel through.

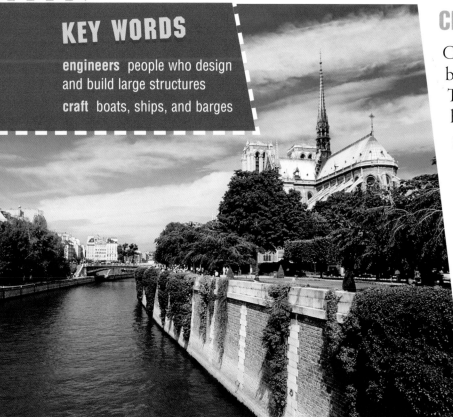

Choosing a route

Choosing a route can be difficult because the canal has to stay level. The route will need to avoid as many hills and valleys as possible, because going over them means building lots of expensive aqueducts, tunnels, and locks. Going around the hills could make the route too long and winding. This is not good if the canal is to transport goods or passengers as quickly and cheaply as possible.

Many old, narrow canals were built to go around hills rather than over or through them. This avoided having to build expensive aqueducts, tunnels, and cuttings to keep the canal level.

The engineers take samples of rocks and soil to test in a laboratory. These tests will tell them if the ground beneath the channel will be easy to dig and how much waterproofing material will be needed.

How wide and how deep?

How wide and how deep the channel should be will depend on the types of **craft** that will use the canal. The surface of a canal is usually six times as wide as the craft that will use it.

A shipping canal is much wider and deeper than a barge canal. The Suez Canal is a shipping canal in Egypt that connects the Mediterranean Sea and the Red Sea. The Suez Canal is more than 820 feet (250 m) across and 65 feet (20 m) deep.

Going up and down

If a canal route needs to go uphill or downhill, locks and inclined planes are used.

Locks

A lock is a short section of canal with a set of gates at each end. The gates have smaller panels in them which can be opened to let water in from the canal above. Doing this raises the water level inside the lock. The water level can be lowered by letting water out of the gates and into the canal below. Instead of gates, some locks have pipes leading from the canal into the lock.

Locks are like a staircase, with each separate lock as a step up or down. If the hill is very long, several locks can be built in a line. Some canals have dozens of locks, which can take several hours to travel through.

Inclined planes

An inclined plane carries a boat up and down a hill inside a gigantic container of water as big as an Olympic swimming pool. Once the boat is inside the container, the container moves slowly along a track, just like a roller-coaster climbing the first slope of the ride.

People on canal boats must be very patient. It takes a lot of time to go through locks or to use an inclined plane.

An inclined plane carries a canal barge down a hill inside a container of water, in Belgium. ▶

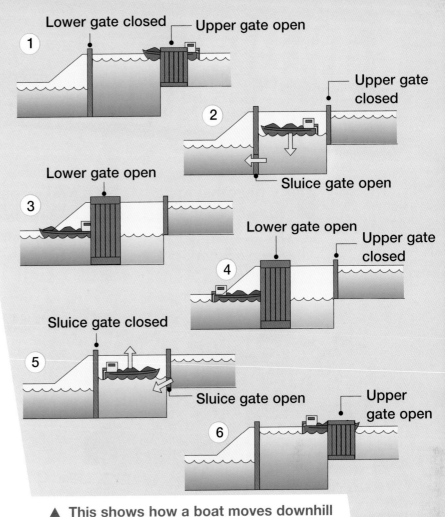

1. Lower gate closed — Upper gate open
2. Upper gate closed — Sluice gate open
3. Lower gate open
4. Lower gate open — Upper gate closed
5. Sluice gate closed — Sluice gate open
6. Upper gate open

▲ This shows how a boat moves downhill through a lock (1, 2, 3) or uphill (4, 5, 6).

BUILDING A CANAL

Once the canal route has been worked out and the bridges, tunnels, aqueducts, cuttings, and locks have been designed, building begins. A new canal might be hundreds of miles long. It is important to have all the machinery in the right places along the canal, ready to be used when it is needed.

Monster diggers

The first canals were dug by hand using simple tools and animals to pull cartloads of earth and rock away. Today, enormous digging machines scoop out millions and millions of tons of soil and rock to dig the channel and cut through smaller hills.

Some of the rock and soil will be pushed into piles by powerful earth-moving machines to make the embankments that will keep the channel level as the land changes. Some will be used to strengthen the canal banks.

If the rock is very hard, explosives are used to shatter it. Explosives are also used to blast a way into rocky hillsides so that tunnel-boring machines can be brought in to dig the tunnels. Tunnel-boring machines have cutting heads with rows of sharp teeth that chew away at the rock as the head spins.

Monster digging machines scoop out the channel using buckets that spin around on a big wheel.

Adding liners and locks

As each section of the canal is dug out, it is lined. A lining might be a thin layer of gravel and stones, or thousands of truckloads of concrete for every mile of the canal. A layer of waterproofing is added afterwards. The canal banks are protected by stones or a mat smeared with asphalt to stop the banks from slipping. Water plants and reeds are planted to protect the banks from being scraped by boats.

Locks

Think of a lock as a huge, watertight, and extremely strong concrete box with a floor and walls several feet thick. While a lock is being built, its earth walls are supported by long steel-and-concrete poles which are driven deep into the ground. Wooden sheets and steel plates are used to make a mold for the concrete to be poured into. A grid of steel bars is placed where the concrete will need to be strengthened. Lock gates are made from steel. They are made in a factory and brought to the lock as they are needed. They hang on enormous hinges in the concrete walls.

The gigantic steel lock gates on the Panama Canal float because they are hollow. This eases the weight on their hinges.

Canalization

Sometimes boats cannot travel quickly and safely through some sections of a river. Craft can detour around rapids, shallow, or winding parts of a river using a system of canals and locks. Water is diverted from the river into a canal alongside it, by building a weir. A weir is a type of low dam that is used to change the direction of the flow of the water or raise the water level. The canal channel is kept straight, level, and deep enough for the craft to travel safely. If the detour means going uphill or downhill, locks are used to raise or lower the water level in the canal, allowing the craft to move up or down. This safer, easier detour is called canalization.

A river channel can also be made deeper and wider, and sharp bends straightened by a special digging machine called a dredger, which works from the bank or a floating barge.

WORKING CANALS AND AQUEDUCTS

Throughout history, canals and aqueducts have been used for transporting goods and as a way to move water from one place to another for different reasons.

Aqueducts

The ancient Romans were great engineers and great users of water! Bathing was an important part of their daily life and huge public baths and fountains were built in every city. The water in many town drinking wells was not clean enough, so a cleaner water supply was needed. Aqueducts were built near where streams and springs could flow into them.

The Romans understood that water always flows downhill and the channel carrying the water was tilted slightly to keep the water moving. Pipes were made of **bronze**, clay, wood, or even leather.

Magnificent tunnels were cut through solid rock. The Romans used fire to heat the rock and cold water to cool it so suddenly that it would crack. Aqueducts were so big that people could stand up inside them. An aqueduct only came out into the open air when it was carried across a valley on great soaring arches.

Some of the water flowed into the town storage tanks. The rest flushed out the toilets.

◀ These tunnels in Morocco are part of an aqueduct system built by the ancient Romans. The arches have been joined together to make them strong enough to support a roof of solid rock.

As the towns and cities grew, it became difficult to keep enough water flowing. The Romans were very clever. It was not too long before they solved the problem by inventing a way to pump the water.

Modern aqueducts

Modern aqueducts are very different from those built by ancient peoples. Modern aqueducts have large, concrete pipes. Concrete is cheap, waterproof, and very strong. The pipes are made in a factory and laid on a bed of gravel or rock pieces in a channel that has been dug by earth-moving machines. The sections of pipe are joined, and the ditch is covered again.

▲ These men are laying the pipes of a modern aqueduct, which will carry water through a city.

The water is collected and stored in a human-made lake, called a reservoir. The water is cleaned and sometimes chemicals are added to it. It is then pushed down the huge main pipe by powerful pumps.

The main water pipe is like a tree trunk, with lots of smaller pipes spreading out from it like branches. The smaller pipes carry the water into different parts of the city. Along the way, more pumps keep the water moving at the same speed. The pumps run on electricity and are controlled by computers. If the water is pumped with too much force, pipes can burst, causing serious flooding. If there is not enough force, the water cannot move uphill.

Water is piped into buildings for people to use, to local swimming centers so the water can be changed regularly in the pool, and to fire hydrants in the street for fire fighters to connect their hoses to. Some water is sent to farms and market gardens to irrigate crops. Other aqueducts carry water to power stations which make a type of electricity from moving water called hydro-electricity.

Transportation canals

In the past, before there were railroads, motor vehicles, or proper roads, canal boats were an important form of inland transportation. Many cities relied on canals for different reasons.

Venice

The city of Venice, in Italy, is famous for its canals. Venice is made up of several islands which sit in a **lagoon** between two rivers near the Adriatic Sea. The old part of the city has no roads at all. Instead, gondolas and motor boats use the 177 canals, just as cars use roads. People cross the canals using the 400 bridges.

◄ The city of Venice, in Italy

The first people to settle in Venice did so because they needed protection from their enemies. Living on the islands made it hard for invading armies to attack them all at once. When the sea came in and out, it washed up between the islands and the enemy ships were smashed into each other or ran aground on the sandbank that protected the lagoon from the sea. As the city grew, these waterways were developed into canals to transport goods from ships into Italy. Today, the canals are a popular tourist attraction. Unfortunately, because Venice is on low-lying land close to the sea, it is often flooded by enormous waves from stormy seas.

KEY WORDS

lagoon an area of seawater separated from the sea by a sandbank or reef

The Netherlands

The Netherlands is another country in Europe which relies on canals. Most of the Netherlands is very flat and low lying. Areas close to the sea are often flooded when powerful storms whip up huge waves. For hundreds of years, the Dutch have used canals, **dikes**, and dams to control flooding.

Canals once transported goods into cities such as Amsterdam and delivered water to water-powered mills. Today, they offer travelers a more relaxed journey into the city instead of using the crowded, narrow streets. Canals have also been used to drain large areas of land so that it can be used for farming or housing.

In the Netherlands, windmills like these were used to power pumps to drain water from the land.

Drainage

The areas in the Netherlands that were being drained were called polders. Poldering meant surrounding a lake with dikes and dams and then pumping it dry. The first pumps had wheels with large scoops on them and were driven by muscle-power. It was very slow and exhausting work for the animals and people working the pumps.

By the 1400s, windmills powered the wheels and the water was pumped into a canal and sent back into the sea or river. In some places, the drainage was so successful that the river or lake eventually shrank to little more than a trickle. With the invention of the steam engine, steam-powered pumps started to be used in the late 1700s. Today, the polders are made by computer-controlled pumps powered by electric motors.

KEY WORDS

dikes thick walls that stop land from becoming flooded by a river or the sea

Industrial canals

Canal networks began to grow rapidly during the **industrial revolution**. Before railroads began to be used, in the 1820s, there was no other way to transport heavy cargo such as coal, grain, wool, and timber. Factories and mills needed a steady supply of coal and timber to keep their machines running. Farmers needed to transport their grain to the mills where it could be ground, and wool and cotton needed to be spun or woven into cloth.

It was impossible to carry such heavy cargo on horse-drawn carts. If these goods were being shipped overseas, a canal network was the only way to bring the goods from the inland factories to the ships waiting in the ports.

◀ **Boats on the canals of London in the 1800s**

Canals were also an important water supply for early industry. Canals supplied water-powered mills with a source of energy to turn their **waterwheels**. When steam-powered machines were invented, water could be drawn from the canals and heated to steam inside boilers.

Even today, some modern canals such as the Moscow–Volga Canal, in Russia, are used as a source of energy to make electricity from moving water. Unfortunately, canals were also seen as a way to remove the waste created by factories and mines. Many canals were polluted with garbage and chemicals.

KEY WORDS

industrial revolution an important time in England, in the late 1700s and early 1800s, when machines were invented and used on farms, in mines, mills, factories, and for transportation, causing enormous changes in the way people lived

waterwheels wheels driven by water which are used to work machinery

Shipping canals

Even though railroads and trucks took over from the canal boats as the main forms of transportation, shipping canals are still very important. Some shipping canals run alongside the coast, slightly inland. They allow ships to travel along the coast without having to tackle storms or dangerous tides and currents. These are called intracoastal waterways. The most important canals are the great shipping canals. These canals shorten the world's sea journeys and make them much safer.

Suez Canal

The Suez Canal is a huge shipping canal in Egypt which links the Mediterranean Sea to the Red Sea. This 104-mile-long (168-km) canal cuts about 3,105 miles (5,000 km) off the journey from northern Europe to Asia, and avoids a long and dangerous trip around Africa. The Suez Canal is one of the world's busiest shipping routes and is especially used by very large oil tankers.

The route

The Suez Canal runs almost in a straight line from Port Said, on the Mediterranean Sea, to the Gulf of Suez, on the Red Sea. It does not take the shortest route between the two seas, but passes through two large lakes, which make up about a quarter of its length.

For most of its length, the channel is only wide enough for one ship. Ships usually travel in a line, one behind the other, but there are four places where ships traveling in the opposite direction can pass each other. Each ship is controlled by a guide, called a pilot, who knows the canal well.

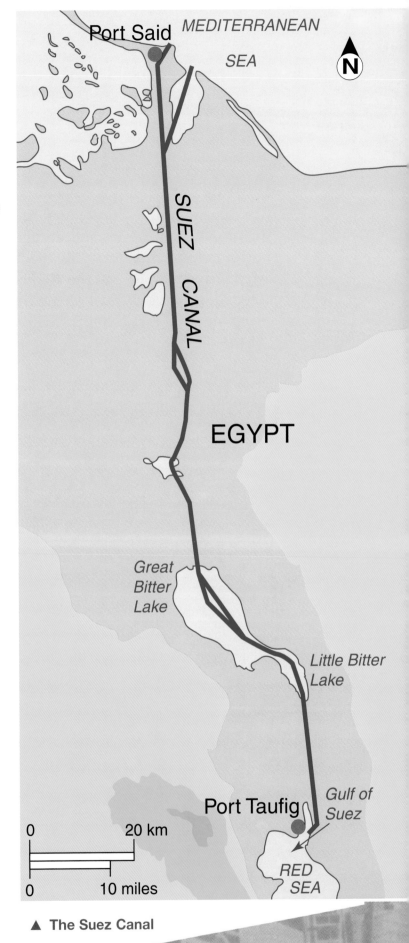

▲ The Suez Canal

Building the Suez Canal

Work began on the Suez Canal in 1859. Most of the digging was done by steam-powered shovels and dredgers which scooped up enough sand from the bottom of the channel to fill 50 Olympic stadiums. The water levels in the Mediterranean Sea and the Red Sea are about the same, so no locks were needed. When the canal opened, in 1869, the channel was 22 feet (7 m) deep and 190 feet (58 m) wide, which was large enough for the steamships of the time.

Eventually, the Suez Canal had to be widened and deepened to allow larger ships through. In 1954, it was widened to 495 feet (151 m) with a depth of 49 feet (15 m). In 1980, it was widened again to 886 feet (270 m) with a depth of 63 feet (19.5 m), making the Suez Canal the deepest canal in the world.

Today, between 15,000 and 20,000 ships pass through the canal each year. Traveling at a speed of 10 miles (16 km) per hour, it takes about 11 to 16 hours to complete the journey. Like many other canals, the Suez is a multi-purpose canal. Water is drawn from it to irrigate crops and provide drinking water for the towns that have grown up along its length.

About 40 to 55 ships pass through the Suez Canal each day.

The Panama Canal

The Panama Canal joins the Atlantic and Pacific oceans across a narrow strip of land in South America, called an isthmus. The canal is 50 miles (81 km) long and cuts the journey from one ocean to the other by one week, or 9,315 miles (15,000 km).

Building the Panama Canal

The canal was built between 1882 and 1914. Special equipment had to be designed to cope with the massive amounts of soil that had to be moved. Railroad wagons with one open side were built so that steam-powered unloaders could reach the soil easily. The unloaders were fast—one unloader could shift soil 300 times faster than one person. An air-powered car called a dirt-spreader followed the unloaders. As the unloaders dropped the soil, the dirt-spreader used steel wings on its sides to smooth it out.

Engineers decided that a canal with locks would be the best design. It took four years to build the three sets of locks. Each enormous lock is three times as long as a soccer field and as deep as a 10-story building. It took enough concrete to fill 600 Olympic swimming pools to build the locks. It would take more than a year to fill each lock from a bath faucet!

◀ A container freight ship making its way through the Miraflores Lock, on the Panama Canal

Using the locks

The lock gates are opened and closed by steel arms, which are connected to giant wheels run by electric motors. Ships are towed through the lock by an electric engine that moves on a track like a train. All the power needed to operate the locks comes from hydro-electricity, which is made using the canal water.

Looking after canals

Canals need to be looked after to keep them in good working order, just like any other structure.

Maintenance

Canals need to be kept clean and clear so that all types of craft can travel safely up and down.

If a bank collapses, it is repaired. If the water level drops, a canal can be topped up from a nearby reservoir or from another canal. If a canal freezes over in winter, an ice-breaking boat is used to clear it.

Dredgers regularly remove any build-up of sand and mud to prevent the channel from becoming too shallow. The dredger has a line of buckets on a moving belt or chain. As the chain or belt turns, the buckets drop onto the channel bottom, digging into the sand. They come up to the surface carrying the sand and dump it when they reach the top. A barge carries all the sand away. Some dredgers use a sucking tube instead of buckets.

> **KEY WORDS**
>
> **foundations** a firm base upon which a structure is built

◄ A bucket dredger has a line of buckets on a cable that scoop up mud and sand from the bottom of the canal.

The different canal structures, such as locks, aqueducts, and tunnels, also need to be checked and, if necessary, repaired. Many tunnels have begun to collapse as the soil around their **foundations** shifts. The brick linings can also peel away. Tunnels under repair have to be closed until they are made safe. The bricks are replaced with strong, hard-wearing concrete linings. Lock gates may need to be replaced. The lock is emptied and the canal closed while the work is carried out.

Canal craft

Canal craft can be small, such as rowing boats and canoes, or massive, such as ocean-going ships. There are barges that carry cargo, and other craft that are designed just for having fun on the water.

Narrowboats

Narrowboats were the first canal boats. They were pushed along using a pole, or pulled by horses. To get through tunnels, the boatman would lie on his back and push against the roofs of tunnels with his feet. Special bridges, with a piece that could be lifted like a castle drawbridge, allowed the horse to pull the towrope through a lock without getting tangled. Narrowboats still run on many British canals because their locks are not very wide.

Barges

Barges are especially designed for use on canals. A barge does not have a **cargo hold** like a ship. A barge carries its cargo on its deck and is much wider than a narrowboat. Most barges have motors. Others, called dumb barges, do not. Dumb barges can be joined together and moved by motorized barges or pulled by a tugboat. A train of dumb barges can carry as much cargo as a large ship.

▲ These dumb barges are being pulled by a tugboat.

Fun

Many old canals that are no longer being used for cargo traffic have been **restored** and are used by people for canal vacations. People can hire boats, walk along the towpaths, or fish from the banks. Some of the old buildings along the canals have been made into museums, and some towns have canal festivals every year.

KEY WORDS

cargo hold the part of a ship where goods are kept during the journey

restored made new again

CANALS THAT WENT WRONG

anals are quite simple structures, but there can still be problems during building. Even when a canal is finished, there could be problems that make it unsafe to use and it must be closed to traffic.

Problems with the Panama Canal

The Panama Canal had many problems during building. The land it passed through was hot, swampy, and infested with mosquitoes. About 20,000 workers died from a disease called yellow fever, which they caught when they were bitten by mosquitoes. The polluted and mosquito-infested swamps were eventually cleaned up. Many workers were injured by accidents involving explosives. The nine-mile-long (15-km) Culebra Cutting took seven years to dig because of landslides. Work began in 1882, and the canal finally opened in 1914.

Trouble in the Suez Canal

In the past, the Suez Canal has been closed because of war. During one war, the canal remained closed for eight years, between 1967 and 1975, because sunken ships blocked it. Cargo ships had to spend several extra days traveling around Africa to reach their destinations.

◄ A sunken freighter boat blocking the Suez Canal in 1967

Leaking canals

The Garagum Canal, in Turkmenistan, is one of the longest canals in the world. This canal is an important source of drinking water and water for irrigation. Unfortunately, most of the canal has never been lined and is leaking into the surrounding soil, making the land boggy and difficult to farm. So much water is being diverted into irrigation that the sea it flows into is drying up.

Canal safety

Many canals are used for water activities such as boating and fishing. Canals can be fun places, but people must be very careful because a canal can also be a very dangerous place. The water is often deep and cold. The steep banks make it very difficult to climb out of the water. Locks are especially dangerous. As a lock fills, the water tumbles violently and can easily flip or flood a small boat. Some canals are still very polluted and swallowing the water can make you ill.

Dry canals can be dangerous

Canals that are used to carry away stormwater to prevent flooding can also be very dangerous. These canals are not completely covered and, although they are nearly always dry, they can become a raging torrent if there is a sudden downpour of heavy rain. Nobody should ever play in these canals. It might be a fine day near the canal, but it could be raining somewhere else, and that water could find its way into the canal, taking everyone by surprise.

▲ Rescue workers in France search a stormwater drain for a little girl who has gone missing.

AMAZING CANALS

anals are some of the world's most amazing structures. Some canals are record-breakers because of their length or depth. Others are amazing because they were built in ancient times with few tools and no modern machinery. Here are some interesting facts and figures—but there are many more you can find out about.

Canals and aqueducts of the past

- The Nahrawan was a canal built in Mesopotamia (now Iraq) more than 5,000 years ago. It was 200 miles (321 km) long and 394 feet (120 m) wide.

- China's Grand Canal was started nearly 2,000 years ago. The 1,107-mile (1,782-km) canal is still in use today. About 5.5 million slave workers built the first section. Two million died from illness, injury, cold, and starvation.

- The Assyrians (who lived in what is now Iraq and Egypt) built an aqueduct 30 feet (10 m) high and 900 feet (274 m) long across a valley. The aqueduct was built from two million large stone blocks.

◄ The ancient Grand Canal in China is still in use today.

Modern aqueducts

- The London Water Ring Main, in England, is a modern aqueduct. It has 50 miles (80 km) of tunnel and supplies 6 million people with 286 million gallons (1,300 million l) of drinking water each day.

- The water supply in New York City comes from three aqueducts. These aqueducts can deliver 1,633 million gallons (6,183 million l) of water each day from sources up to 120 miles (193 km) away.

Locks

Locks are a feature of many canals. When you know that an Olympic swimming pool is 164 feet (50 m) long and 65 feet (20 m) wide, you can work out how many swimming pools would fit into each lock.

Longest and widest

- The Berendrecht Lock in Antwerp, Belgium, is 1,641 feet (500 m) long and 223 feet (68 m) wide.
- The Mississippi System, in the U.S., is 1,191 feet (363 m) long and 108 feet (33 m) wide.
- The Panama Canal is 984 feet (300 m) long and 108 feet (33 m) wide.

Longest and deepest canal structures

Deepest lock
The Zhaporozhe Lock, Ukraine, is 122 feet (37.4 m) deep.

Longest lock staircase
The Tardebigge, Worcester, and Birmingham Canal, in England, has 30 locks.

Longest inclined plane
The inclined plane in Ronquieres, Belgium, raises boats 219 feet (67 m). Its length is 38,057 feet (11,600 m) and the maximum barge size is 1,488 tons (1,350 t).

Longest canal tunnel
The canal tunnel in Rôve, France, on the Marseilles–Rhône Canal, is 4.4 miles (7.1 km) long. It was opened in 1853.

The length of the world's major shipping canals	
Suez Canal, Egypt (completed 1869)	104 miles (168 km)
Kiel Canal, Germany (completed 1895)	62 miles (99 km)
Panama Canal, Panama (completed 1914)	50 miles (81 km)
Manchester Ship Canal, England (completed 1894)	35 miles (57 km)
Corinth Canal, Greece (completed 1893)	4 miles (7 km)

USING MODELS TO LEARN ABOUT STRUCTURES

You can find out about some of the challenges engineers meet when they design and build a canal or aqueduct by using a construction set to build your own. Construction sets have everything needed to build a canal. Think carefully about the shapes that you will need to use. Remember, a canal has to stay level. You may need to build some canal structures such as locks, tunnels, and bridges.

Strength and stability are just as important in a construction set as they are in a life-sized structure. Many of today's engineers and architects started with construction sets. They are still building with them—the construction sets just grew bigger.

Construction sets are a great way to learn about strong and stable canals and aqueducts. ▼

GLOSSARY

alloy	a mixture of two or more metals
barges	flat-bottomed boats used on canals
bronze	a yellowish metal that is a mixture of copper and tin
cargo hold	the part of a ship where goods are kept during the journey
cement	an ingredient in concrete which makes the concrete harden like stone
channel	a ditch along which water is carried
concrete	a building material made by mixing cement and sand or gravel with water
craft	boats, ships, and barges
cuttings	passages that have been dug through a hill
dikes	thick walls that stop land from becoming flooded by a river or the sea
embankments	human-made mounds of earth that support a canal
engineers	people who design and build large structures
flexible	able to bend without breaking
foundations	a firm base upon which a structure is built
gondola	a long, narrow boat pushed forward by a pole
industrial revolution	an important time in England, in the late 1700s and early 1800s, when machines were invented and used on farms, in mines, mills, factories, and for transportation, causing enormous changes in the way people lived
lagoon	an area of seawater separated from the sea by a sandbank or reef
locks	steps on a canal that let boats move uphill or downhill
materials	anything used to make a structure
mills	buildings where grain is crushed to make flour
piers	upright columns on which arches rest
reinforced	made stronger
restored	made new again
sewage	dirty water and waste from toilets
structure	something that is made up of many parts joined together
vertical	standing upright
watertight	not leaking
waterwheels	wheels driven by water which are used to work machinery

INDEX